Reptile Keeper's Guides

Leopard and Fat-Tailed Geckos

R. D. Bartlett
Patricia P. Bartlett

BARRON'S

Acknowledgments

Throughout the years, we have had the great pleasure of meeting many other gecko enthusiasts and learning what works (and what does not) for them. They have all been generous with their time and knowledge. In particular, we would like to thank Bill and Marcia Brant and Joe Hiduke of The Gourmet Rodent; Denice Ferrara and Mark Baldel of Golden Gecko; Mark Leshock and Kim Harding of Mark Leshock Reptiles; Rob MacInnes and Mike Stuhlman of Glades Herp; and Rich and Connie Zuchowski of SerpenCo. We would also like to thank Ron Tremper for his photos on pages 12 (top), 31 (top and bottom), 32, 33 (middle and bottom), 43, 44, and 45, and Zig Leszczynski for his photos on page 5 (top), 9 (bottom), 23 (top and bottom), 35, and 41.

All inquiries should be addressed to:
Barron's Educational Series, Inc.
250 Wireless Boulevard
Hauppauge, NY 11788
www.barronseduc.com

Library of Congress Catalog Card No. 2008044404

ISBN-13: 978-0-7641-4095-2
ISBN-10: 0-7641-4095-7

Library of Congress Cataloging-in-Publication Data
Bartlett, Richard D., 1938–
    Leopard and fat-tailed geckos / R.D. Bartlett, Patricia Bartlett. — 2nd ed.
        p. cm. — (Reptile keeper's guides)
    Includes bibliographical references and index.
    ISBN-13: 978-0-7641-4095-2 (alk. paper)
    ISBN-10: 0-7641-4095-7 (alk. paper)
    1. Leopard geckos as pets. I. Bartlett, Patricia Pope, 1949–. II. Title.

SF459.G35B386 2009
639.3'952—dc22   2008044404

Printed in China
9 8 7 6 5 4 3 2 1

Contents

Introduction

Without question, the leopard gecko is now the most commonly bred lizard in the United States and among the most popular in Europe and Asia as well. Although the fat-tailed gecko is not yet as popular in breeding programs, it displays many of the same gentle, winning characteristics as the leopard gecko. Both are pretty, are small in size, adapt well to terraria as small as 10 or 15 gallons (38 or 57 l) in size, are very hardy, and require little specialized support equipment. They are active at night when their owners are most likely to be at home. In short, no lizard pet is better than a leopard or fat-tailed gecko for beginning hobbyists. Breeding programs for color morphs assure that both lizards will hold the interest of their keepers for many years to come.

This is the coloration of an adult leopard gecko collected from the wild. From this, through selective breeding, have come all other colors and patterns.

Hatchling leopard geckos of normal or wild coloration.

What Are Leopard and Fat-Tailed Geckos?

Leopard and fat-tailed geckos are members of the gecko family, Eublepharidae. This is a primitive gecko family containing primarily terrestrial members that share such characteristics as well-developed and fully functional eyelids and toes without expanded toe tips (typical geckos lack eyelids, and most have expanded toe tips). Eublepharines have vertically elliptical pupils, which expand greatly in the darkness. Not too surprisingly, both the leopard and the fat-tailed geckos are nocturnal.

Eublepharines share other characteristics. All have the caudal (tail) scales arranged in prominent whorls. A noticeable constriction occurs at the tail base; the tail will break off (auto-tomise) quite easily at that point. The tail regrows (regenerates) quickly, but the regenerated tail differs from the original in both shape and color.

Most eublepharine geckos are prominently banded (at least when young) in yellow or straw and in purplish, brown, or black. The overall pattern of leopard geckos diffuses with advancing age. When fully adult, the leopard gecko is intricately spotted or reticulated with yellow and black. The fully adult fat-tailed gecko always retains its white-edged cross bands of dark brown against a background of pinkish tan.

Eublepharine geckos are widespread. They commonly live in semiarid and arid habitats of the

This is a beautiful pair of normal-colored fat-tailed geckos.

This is another pretty leopard gecko of unknown genetic lineage.

southwestern United States, much of Mexico and northern Central America, Japan (including some of its islands), southeast Asia, and eastern Africa. Once thought to be the most primitive member of the family, the cat gecko, *Aeluroscalabotes felinus*, is now in a family of its own.

The leopard gecko is scientifically designated *Eublepharis macularius*. It is indigenous to Pakistan and India. It is a big-headed, heavy-bodied lizard that may reach a length of 9 inches (23 cm). Its African counterpart, the fat-tailed gecko, is designated *Hemitheconyx caudicinctus*. Fat-tails, as they are commonly called, are from dry, tropical West Africa. A fully adult male may grow to slightly more than 8 inches (20 cm). Fat-tails are very apt to shed their tails when handled and so must never be lifted by their tails. In contrast, the leopard geckos, if gently handled, can be lifted by their tails (although we advise against this). Tail loss or autotomy, as mentioned earlier, is well-known in eublepharine geckos (and in lizards of many other families).

Some of the tail vertebrae of the eublepharine geckos contain fracture planes—slightly weakened areas at which the tail breaks when stressed. The tail may actually break more readily at its thickest point (mid-length) or closer to the body than at its tip, and the tail of the fat-tailed gecko is far more fragile than the tail of the leopard gecko. This may seem surprising, because the tail of a well-nourished male adult fat-tailed gecko may be more than 1.25 inches (3.2 cm) wide at the thickest point. A tail break is accompanied by surprisingly little bleeding, for the blood vessels are also specialized and seal nearly immediately when the tail is broken. The process of regeneration occurs rapidly. Replacement tail growth may be seen within a few weeks. Although certainly not desirable, should it occur, tail loss is not life threatening to the lizard. In fact, just the opposite is true. If a predator grabs the gecko's tail, escape is possible for the lizard. The autotomy of the tail has unquestionably saved the lives of innumerable lizards, leopard and fat-tailed geckos included.

Both species use their tail in signaling, especially when hunting. When prowling, the leopard gecko usually curls its tail upward or to the side and

may wag it to and fro as it walks or runs. In like manner, when the fat-tailed gecko is nervous or hunting, it elevates its tail and waves it sinuously. The exact function of tail waggling is not known, but it may serve to distract some prey or predator species.

In the wild, the secretive leopard gecko inhabits dry desert areas or semi-arid areas such as where the desert meets the savanna. During the day, it seeks cover beneath rocks, in burrows of its own making, or in those abandoned by rodents. The fat-tailed gecko lives in rocky wood-lands and savannas. It is adept at secluding itself beneath available sur-face debris or in uninhabited burrows. Socialization dynamics and caging requirements for the two are different enough so it is best if they are not housed together. However, by provid-ing correct caging, hide boxes, and food, both of these geckos live long lives in captivity. The leopard gecko commonly lives 15 to 22 years; the fat-tailed gecko lives 15 years or more.

The males of both of these lizards vocalize. They most often voice their repertoire of quiet squeaks or clicks during territory disputes.

Prekilled pinky mice are often relished as an occasional treat, as shown by this pretty male albino tangerine fat-tailed gecko.

Geckos as Pets

Selecting Your Gecko

If given good care, leopard and fat-tailed geckos are wonderful and usually long-lived lizards. If you choose yours carefully the chances are that both you and your pet will be together for a long time.

When choosing your gecko, you must consider the size of the food insects available. If only adult crickets are available, you will not want to start with a hatchling gecko. Have your food sources fully figured out before getting your gecko. The source of your gecko is important, too. If you have a choice between a wild-collected or a captive-bred and hatched specimen, choose the latter. It will be less likely to harbor untenable infestations of endoparasites. In addition, it will probably be better acclimated to

captive conditions than would a wild-collected specimen. Finally, and this might sound like a rather minor consideration, if you purchase a captive-bred and hatched specimen, it is a positive statement for herpetoculture and a positive step for conservation.

The leopard or fat-tailed gecko you select should be stocky, be alert, be active (if gently prodded), have all of its fingers and toes, not have open wounds, and not have sunken eyes. Whether you select one with a broken or regenerated tail will be largely up to you. Neither of these conditions is harmful to the gecko, but keep in mind that regenerated tails are never as attractive as the gecko's original tail. Do not select an obviously undernourished gecko. Gently urge it to walk onto your hand, then cup your other hand over it, and grasp it around the neck and body. (You want to look at its ventral side, and this is the best way to pick up a gecko.) Look at the animal's vent. Feces smeared at the vent or signs of loose stools within the enclosure itself are signs of digestive or parasitic problems. If the gecko you select has been collected from the wild, you should consider having fecal smears tested by a veterinarian to

The banded geckos of the genus *Coleonyx* are the North American representatives of the family Eublepharidae. Pictured is the San Diegan banded gecko, *Coleonyx variegatus abbottii*.

determine the type and load of gut parasites.

Captive-breeding programs are able to supply the demand for leopard geckos and can almost supply the demand for fat-tailed geckos. This speaks well not only for the hardiness and adaptability of the lizards but for the ever-increasing knowledge and diligence of hobbyists and commercial reptile breeders or herpetoculturists. Indeed, largely due to the promotional efforts of these enthusiasts, leopard (and fat-tailed geckos) have attained the immense popularity that they now enjoy in the reptile-keeping hobby.

Obtaining Your Gecko

You can obtain leopard and fat-tailed geckos in many ways. They are available at many pet stores, from specialty dealers, at captive breeder expos, or from the breeders themselves. Let's explore some of these avenues of acquisition.

Pet Stores

We advocate purchasing from pet stores because of their convenience and because customers can discuss the gecko in which they are interested on a one-to-one basis with a knowledgeable store employee. This discussion can easily cover topics such as routine care. If problems come up later (and they shouldn't), customers have someone to talk to. The pet store cannot be expected to know some things. These topics include the origin of a given wild-collected specimen and the history and genetics of either normal-appearing or aberrant captive-bred specimens. Remember, the local pet shop is often two or even three or four times removed from the initial

Hatchlings (top) and adult (bottom) snow leopard geckos.

dealing that placed the specimen into the pet trade. Unfortunately, the information given, whether accurate or erroneous, is often self-perpetuating. When giving information about the source of the animal to a new hobbyist, it would benefit all if conversations began with, "Our supplier tells us. . . ."

Reptile and Amphibian Expos

Herp expos came into being about two decades ago. They are now held in many larger cities across the United States and are becoming popular in Europe. Seemingly, at least one occurs at some point in the United States on

When hatchlings, leopard geckos look very much like North American banded geckos.

fecundity, health, or quirks of the species with which they work and especially of the specimens in their breeding programs.

Some breeders are content just to produce geckos. Others, such as Bill and Marcia Brant of The Gourmet Rodent, Inc. in Gainesville, Florida, produce not only thousands of leopard and fat-tailed geckos of traditional color morphs but selectively breed both for enhanced colors and patterns as well. Mark Leshock of Mark Leshock Reptiles in Perkasie, Pennsylvania, specializes in particular traits such as albinism in leopard geckos and leucistic and designer morph fat-tailed geckos.

any given weekend. Some are annual events, others may occur biannually or quarterly. An expo is merely a gathering of dealers and breeders all under one roof. Expos vary in size from the 450-plus tables of the National Reptile Breeders' Expo in Orlando, Florida to some that are much smaller but nearly as comprehensive. Leopard and fat-tailed geckos, in all existing colors, are popular expo items.

Breeders

Breeders may vary in size from backroom hobbyists who produce only a few leopard or fat-tailed geckos every year to commercial breeders who produce literally thousands of hatchlings. With each passing year, more and more breeders present the fruits of their labors at herp expos, but many do not. These other breeders often advertise in your local newspaper or in the classified or pictorial ads sections in specialty reptile and amphibian magazines (see Helpful Information, page 45). Breeders usually offer parasite-free, well-acclimated specimens and accurate information. Most keep records of genetics, lineage,

Specialty Dealers

Due to the continuing growth in popularity of reptiles, specialty dealers have sprung up throughout the reptile-breeding world. Besides often breeding fair numbers of the reptiles they offer, specialty dealers deal directly with other breeders (across the world) and may even be direct importers. Imported specimens are usually acclimated, have been fed, and have often been subjected to a veterinary checkup. Many such dealers both buy and sell reptiles and amphibians at herp expos.

Mail-order Purchase and Shipping

Despite today's proliferation of herp expos and chain pet stores, leopard and fat-tailed geckos and the expos are still not readily available to many small-town hobbyists. Mail order may be the best way to secure the geckos in which you are interested. Here are a few simple guidelines for accomplishing such a purchase.

The African clawed gecko, *Holodactylus africanus*, is a small, strictly nocturnal eublepharine that can be difficult to acclimate to captive conditions.

- **World Wide Web.** By instructing your search engine to seek *leopard geckos* or *fat-tailed geckos*, you should learn the names of dozens of breeders and suppliers. Many web sites provide excellent photos.

- **Classified ads.** Dealers and hobbyists list their available livestock in the classified ads of reptile and amphibian magazines and of pet magazines.

- **Word of mouth.** Ask friends and fellow enthusiasts for recommendations about the reptile dealers they know. Try to check on reliability by asking about dealers at nature centers, museums, zoos, or hobbyist groups.

  The shipping of reptiles is not the insurmountable barrier that many hobbyists initially think it to be. However, shipping can be expensive. Your chosen supplier will be familiar with shipping methods and will assist you in any way possible. You and your shipper will have to agree about the

This is a beautiful male albino fat-tailed gecko.

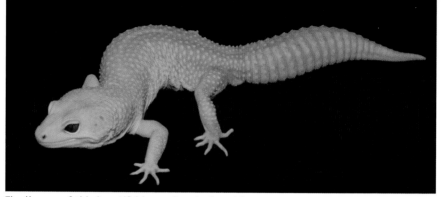

The lineage of this beautiful leopard gecko is not known.

method of payment, the method and date of shipping, and other details.

Payment to the shipper will often include all handling and shipping charges. The payment method should be agreed upon and fully understood by both you and the shipper at the time of ordering. Unless the shipper knows you well, he or she will almost always insist that all charges due be paid for in full prior to shipping. Most dealers accept credit cards, Pay-Pal, money orders, wire transfer of funds, or cashier's checks. Some shippers will accept personal checks but will not ship until the check has cleared their bank (usually a week or so after depositing it). Lizards may be shipped by a few methods.

- They may be shipped by the U.S. Postal Service via Express Mail, a door-to-door or post office–to–post office service. The cost is usually between $25 and $40.

- Express shipping companies, such as DHL, FedEx, or UPS, will accept lizards. Charges are between $25 and $55 for this door-to-door service.

Remember that someone must be at your home to sign for any of the door-to-door services.

Your supplier will need your full name, address, and current day and night telephone numbers. After the first time, it is likely that you will no longer consider the shipping process to be a daunting experience.

Originally considered a divergent eublepharine, the arboreal Malaysian cat gecko, *Aeluroscalabotes felinus*, was recently given its own subfamily, Aeluroscalabotinae.

Caging

Since leopard and fat-tailed geckos are rather small (actually they are big for geckos!) and not overly active, their terraria can be relatively small. Since they are nocturnal animals, you do not need to worry about adding light to the cages. Simply ensure that the temperatures are warm enough. Although we prefer to provide them with larger quarters, a terrarium made from a 10-gallon (38-l) tank is sufficiently large for one male and one or two female leopard geckos. Fat-tails require slightly more space. To create a bare-bones cage, you can use a plastic sweater or blanket box. A shoe box can house one gecko. A trio of leopard geckos can live in a sweater box. A blanket box will work for a trio of fat-tailed geckos.

The substrate for your geckos may consist of 1 or 2 inches (3 to 5 cm) of fine desert sand, small pebbles, cypress mulch, or other absorbent material. Newspaper would work in a pinch, but it does not offer enough purchase to give your pet adequate footing. Paper towels offer footing and are very absorbent.

An important aspect of your caging is hiding areas or hide boxes. Provide enough cork bark or similar hiding places so each gecko can claim at least one. Geckos with insufficient food or hide boxes tend to feel stressed and lose weight.

Although your nocturnal geckos do not need light for heat, they do need warm temperatures. For the leopard gecko in its desert cage and for the fat-tailed gecko in its savanna terrarium, this means daytime temperatures of 80 to 85°F (26.7 to 29.4°C) with nighttime temperatures from 70 to 75°F (21.1 to 23.9°C). An undertank heater is the easiest way to supply this sort of heat. If you put the pad under only one end of the tank and provide hide boxes at each end, your gecko can move to the cooler box at night or as it desires. If you use a standard aquarium as your terrarium, you can add a light at the screen top so you can see your pet(s) more clearly. A red bulb is best to observe your geckos at night.

Add a water dish. Your pet will need clean water available at all times. Remember to add a few pebbles, marbles, or a small stick if you feed crickets to your gecko so the crickets will not drown.

A portrait of a pretty fat-tailed gecko.

The Terrarium for the Leopard Gecko

Leopard geckos are even-tempered, rather social creatures who will live together in small groups if only one male is in each group. The substrate of the desert terrarium can be smooth sand or small rocks. Both are available in pet stores. The depth of the substrate can vary. If you use only a fine covering, your tank will, of course, be lighter and easier to move and handle. If you use a thick layer, be certain that the stand on which your terrarium sits can hold the weight.

Over the years, we have noted concerns about the use of sand as a substrate. The principal concern seems to be the possibility of intestinal impaction if a gecko ingests the sand. However, for the more than 40 years that we have kept and bred herpetofauna, we have never lost a lizard nor even had a serious problem from impaction. After all, what is a desert if not sand? Multiple factors may also intervene to prevent impaction in the wild. A wild amphibian or reptile has a far more active lifestyle than that of even the best kept captive. Normal hydration, a normal diet, and a metabolism elevated by a normal activity pattern probably assist in moving accidentally ingested sand through the digestive system of a wild specimen.

However, we will be the first to admit that different types of sand exist. If the chance of sand-related problems does worry you, we urge you to use a smooth-grained desert sand (several brands are now available), not a sharp-grained silica play sand, in your terrarium.

The top of your desert terrarium should be made of screen. This will prevent a buildup of cage humidity.

Cage Furniture

Rock ledges and caves, individual basking rocks, potted arid-land plants, cork bark hiding areas, and cholla cactus skeletons can be provided for both decoration and the psychological well-being of your specimen(s).

You can affix rocks and, occasionally, cork bark, to the back and/or side glass of the terrarium. Lightweight plastic rock backgrounds are available that offer dozens of small lookout and concealment areas. These treatments can offer additional beauty, complex-

The non-annulated, turniplike regenerated tail of this adult fat-tailed gecko is typical in appearance of the regenerated tails of both leopard and fat-tailed geckos.

Pretty is as pretty does! Although the genetics of many leopard geckos may be unknown, as shown here this often in no way affects their beauty.

ity, and balance to your desert terrarium, and provide a feeling of naturalness and security to the lizard inhabitants. Any and all rocks (and other components) used in a terrarium ledge must be fixed both to each other and to the aquarium glass against which they are stacked. Clear silicone aquarium sealant is often used for this purpose. Do not depend on the integrity of the sealant alone. Rather, build your ledge carefully, depending on the materials to support each other. Consider the sealant as only a part of the system that prevents the terrarium inhabitants from moving or dislodging rocks. Apply the sealant liberally, but also assure that it is not visible when the terrarium is viewed from the front. Be absolutely certain that any hides or planters built into the ledge have sufficient integrity to withstand the rigors of time and the efforts of the inhabitants to dislodge them. Periodically check the integrity of the ledges, and reaffix them as necessary.

Desert Plants

You must pay as much attention to the choice of plants for your terrarium as you do the selection of your geckos.

Choose plants that fit the dimensions of your terrarium. Remember that the nearer the tip of a leaf is to an incandescent lightbulb, the more light and warmth it receives. Thus, although the top of a sansevieria leaf may receive sufficient light for proper growth, the leaf may be severely burned by the heat from the bulb. Choose and position plants and any overhead bulbs sympathetically. Also, choose and utilize plants according to the intensity of the light you can provide. Be ready to change plant species if necessary from those requiring high light situations to species demanding less if growth becomes spindly or discolored. Many species and cultivars of common and easily grown cacti and succulents are available. Many grow well under intense artificial lighting, and some flower freely under such conditions. Plant grow bulbs are better for your plants than cool white or other more commonly used household bulbs.

Cacti: Despite their obvious armament, we have used cacti in our terraria over the decades and have never had any problems. Among those that grow well include the genus *Mammillaria*; several of the less lethally armed fishhook cacti,

13

Setting Up a Desert Terrarium _____

Choose a tank of suitable and adequate size. A 15- to 20-gallon (57 to 76 l) long tank will suffice. Note that the larger the tank, the more forgiving it is of errors and oversights. Be certain that the stand on which the terrarium will sit can safely hold the weight.
Materials needed:

1. Terrarium and stand
2. Substrates; fine upper layer (sand) and coarse lower layer (pea-sized river rock)
3. Drought-tolerant plants (cacti and succulents)
4. Rocks and/or other terrarium furniture (contorted grape and manzanita branches, cholla skeletons, cork bark [both flat and tubular sections], water receptacle) and camouflaged hide boxes
5. A piece of air-conditioning filter material the length and width of the terrarium or enough plastic screening to fold into two layers between the two substrates
6. Non-toxic sealant for holding rocks or heavy cage furniture safely in place.
7. Undertank heater
8. Terrarium top (metal-framed screen or wire top is best; full glass tops are not acceptable)
9. Lighting fixtures and bulbs (plant bulbs are best)
10. Small ventilation fan (optional)

Setup procedure:

1. Place the tank onto its stand with the undertank heater in place (follow the directions carefully when placing and connecting the heaters).
2. Place and seal any heavy cage furniture (rocks, limbs, etc.) in place. This is a particularly important step. If these items just lie atop the surface sand, your geckos can burrow beneath them, allowing the rocks to settle on them. This can injure or kill the animals. Allow a minimum of 24 hours for the sealant to cure.
3. Place the pea-sized river rock on the bottom of the tank to the depth desired (we suggest 2 to 3 inches [5 to 8 cm]).
4. Lay the air-conditioning filter material atop the gravel. (Using a double thickness of plastic window screening will also suffice.)

5. Pour the fine sand on top of the filter material (or screen) to the desired depth. Again, we suggest creating a depth of several inches. If you prefer a textured surface, you can mix a few pieces of variably sized river rock with the sand. Be sure that undertank heaters have a liberal thickness of sand covering them.

6. Place the plants where you wish them. We prefer to leave the plants in their pots and sink the pots to the rim in the sand. This retains the moisture (and plant food) better when the plants are watered. It also prevents extensive areas of sand from becoming overly moist or saturated with fertilizer. If the plants begin suffering from insufficient light or other growth problems, simply replace them.

Alternatively, you can remove the plants from their pots and plant them directly into the sand. You must then use extreme care when watering and fertilizing. Replacing the plants will be more difficult.

7. Arrange any remaining lightweight cage furniture either on the sand surface or partially buried in the sand, as desired. Depending on the number and compatibility of the specimens to be kept in the tank, include from one to several secure hide boxes/hiding areas.

8. If you use artificial lighting, position and affix the fixtures. Since leopard geckos are nocturnal, the use of lighting is optional for a terrarium devoid of plants.

This is a pretty, adult-striped phase, fat-tailed gecko.

Ferocactus; star cacti, *Astrophytum*; and the comparatively spineless beaver-tail cacti, which are cultivars of the genus *Opuntia*. (The use of cacti with recurred spines—such as *Ferocactus* sp.—in a lizard terrarium is contraindicated.)

Euphorbias: Euphorbias are the old-world counterpart of cacti. Members of the genus *Euphorbia* vary from tree-sized succulents that drip quantities of a quite toxic, latex-like sap when injured to tiny spherical tennis ball-sized species that are ideally suited for a desert terrarium. Other examples include the varied crowns of thorns, which, despite their spiny aspect, make fine terrarium plants when small. Like cacti, many euphorbias are readily available in nurseries and garden shops. Most of the smaller euphorbias will grow well under dry terrarium conditions, but few produce significant flowers.

Haworthias and Gasterias: These are commonly grown nursery plants that readily cluster into impressive, dwarfed thickets. Most of these lily relatives have leaves tipped with a rather weak spine and have weakly serrated, spiny leaf edges. Of the two genera, the haworthias seem the easier to cultivate. They require little in the way of winter cooling. The gasterias, on the other hand, do enjoy cooler and drier conditions during the short days of winter. Most of the commonly offered species in both genera will grow well in somewhat less light than will most cacti and euphorbias.

Sansevierias: These are ideal moderate- to high-light terrarium plants available in a myriad of species and cultivars. Some are so tall that they will be suitable only for the tallest terraria. Others are dwarfed and form attractive, clustered rosettes of green. For those enthusiasts who like a little variety in terrarium plants, many of the sansevierias are available in both normal and variegated forms.

The Terrarium for the Fat-Tailed Gecko

Like leopard geckos, fat-tailed geckos are not overly active. However, fat-tails are more solitary than leopard geckos. It is best, therefore, to keep them either singly or in small groups of not more than three—one male and two females—to an enclosure. Also, the enclosure for a trio should not have less floor space than that provided by a 15-gallon (57-l) aquarium (12 by 24 inches; 30 by 61 cm). We feel that a 20-gallon (76-l) tank (12 by 30 inches; 30 by 76 cm) or larger would be better. At least one secure hiding area must be provided for each lizard, even though all geckos will sometimes use the same one.

Fat-tailed geckos need slightly higher humidity than the more arid-adapted leopard geckos. The substrate

Note the prominent ear opening and functional eyelids in this leopard gecko portrait.

This is an adult patternless (leucistic) leopard gecko.

for the savanna terrarium can be bark nuggets, a medium that promotes a reasonably high cage humidity. You can, of course, use other substrates. However, if you use a dry or desiccating substrate, you may have to mist the fat-tail's cage every day or two. Too little humidity can result in your fat-tailed gecko(s) refusing to feed and having difficulty shedding.

Building a Savanna Terrarium

The extremes of weather and the seasonality of the savanna's plant life (especially the grasses) make savanna habitats difficult to reproduce. To add to the challenge, typical savanna plants such as esparto grass (*Stipa tenacissima*) and Copernicus palms are rarely available in nurseries or garden shops. You are likely to find yourself literally grasping at straws—or at least dead grasses—to complete the design.

Plants for the Savanna Terrarium

Unless you have a conservatory or greenhouse that you can devote to the task, growing the various species of perennial thorn scrub will be an impossibility. Even should you succeed, only the smallest seedlings would fit into an indoor terrarium; however, some rather easily grown succulents can take the place of the scrub in the terrarium.

The many species and cultivars of snake plant or sansevieria are ideal for brilliantly lighted savanna or desert tanks. These are African plants that have been naturalized in many other areas of the world. Many are popular houseplants. Some species have interesting cylindrical leaves, others have curious spatulate leaves, and yet others have normal leaves that form short, ground-hugging rosettes. Those with which most of us are familiar have sturdy straplike leaves from 8 to 36 inches (20 to 91 cm) in height. The sansevierias are both hardy and drought tolerant. They can be propagated by offsets, by rooting leaf cuttings, and, more rarely, by seed. As expected, the plants need more water during their periods of active growth than during dormancy.

Setting Up a Savanna Terrarium

Choose a 20- to 30-gallon (76 to 114 l) terrarium for your fat-tails. They need slightly more room than leopard geckos do.
Materials needed:

1. Terrarium and stand
2. Top and lighting fixtures
3. Aquarium sealant to affix rocks and limbs if necessary
4. Styrofoam insert 2 inches (5 cm) thick and, as long as the terrarium but of variable width
5. Small Phillips head screwdriver or ice pick to make holes (in which grasses will stand) in the Styrofoam
6. Dried grasses
7. Potted drought-tolerant plants
8. Rocks, limbs, grapevines, cholla skeletons, and so forth and also a water receptacle
9. Pea-sized gravel for bottommost substrate
10. Cypress mulch, bark nuggets, or perhaps smooth sand (such as desert sand); do not use sharp silica play sand
11. Air-conditioning filter material (to partition sand from gravel)
12. Undertank heater

Setup procedure:

1. Position the stand and terrarium in the chosen area.
2. Position the undertank heater.
3. Cut the Styrofoam insert to the length of the cage and as wide as desired. This will hold your grass stems and perhaps some of your potted plants unless you simply bury the pots in the mulch or bark. Place the Styrofoam onto the floor of the tank.
4. Fill areas of the tank not covered by Styrofoam with about 2 inches (5 cm) of pea-sized gravel.
5. Cut the air-conditioning filter material to the necessary shape, and lay it on top of the gravel.
6. Position and seal heavy cage furniture (rocks, heavy logs, and so on) in place with nontoxic sealant. Many sealants do not adhere to Styrofoam, so affix the furniture to the back and end glass of the terrarium. Let the sealant cure (this may take 24 hours).
7. Position the potted plants where desired. You can carve holes out of the Styrofoam where necessary to accept the pots.

8. Punch holes in the Styrofoam with the Phillips head screwdriver or ice pick where desired, and insert the grass stems.

9. Carefully add mulch/bark/sand (the grass stems are easily bent) to the desired depth over the air-conditioning material and Styrofoam. Thoroughly fill in around the grass stems, potted plants, and cage furniture.

10. Place the screen top onto the tank. If using any live plants, add a plant grow bulb, suitably positioning and affixing it so the beam falls onto the plants.

11. Add a water dish to the end of the tank farther away from the undertank heater.

12. As with all other terraria, we suggest that you opt for the largest tank that you can afford and accommodate. Large terraria are easier to design and maintain than smaller ones.

The differences between normal (top) and albino (bottom) are easily seen in these hatchling fat-tailed geckos.

The Gourmet Rodent bred this tangerine striped albino leopard gecko.

Succulents such as *Haworthia* (left) and *Gasteria* (right) are excellent, small, and hardy terrarium plants. To thrive they will need strong daytime lighting.

The tennis ball-shaped and -sized *Euphorbia globosa* is an interesting and very hardy plant that will adapt well to a savanna terrarium. Smaller species of *Pachypodium*, spiny succulents from Africa and Madagascar, adapt well to the savanna terrarium. Sadly, the species most often grown in pots—*P. lamerei*—attains treelike proportions. The smallest species, *P. brevicaule*, is a cactiform species that is a remarkable

This subadult leopard gecko may develop into a beautiful overall tangerine.

rock-mimic with sparse leaves but beautiful yellow flowers. In addition to these are several ideal species of moderate size, differing structure, and superb hardiness, including *P. bispinosum* and *P. succulentum*.

Calibanus hookeri is a strange Mexican caudiciform plant (the ecological equivalent of cactus) that has numerous discrete tufts of raspy-surfaced grassy leaves emerging from the caudex. It is hardy and, in small sizes, ideal for the savanna terrarium.

Most of the various wart or star plants of the genus *Haworthia* thrive amid the rocks in a savanna terrarium. Some have comparatively tender leaves, while the leaves of others are tough and almost indestructible. These plants have rosettes of leaves and may either be a squat, rather broadly opened rosette or be rather tall with the leaves clasping the stem.

Nurseries sell purslane or portulaca for hanging garden baskets and as bedding plants. They are fragile, drought-tolerant succulents and require very bright lighting. Because they are inexpensive and bear beautiful blossoms, these plants are occasionally used as expendable terrarium plants.

Feeding

Diet

In the wild, leopard and fat-tailed geckos feed on all manner of nonnoxious insects, including hard-shelled beetles and their larvae, spiders, scorpions, and other arthropods. If they find a nest, these geckos may occasionally consume a newborn mouse.

As captives, leopards and fat-tails will thrive on a diet of crickets (both black and gray), common and giant mealworms, and occasionally wax worms. They may eagerly accept an occasional pinky mouse, especially the adult male geckos. If a grassy or shrubby area not treated with insecticides is available, you can augment your gecko's diet with insects caught there in a sweep net. Not only do geckos relish such things as moths, roaches, sow bugs, and hairless caterpillars, but wild insects generally contain more nutrition than domestically raised ones. A varied diet is best. Tailor the size of the food items offered to the size of your lizard(s).

You should dust food insects weekly with a calcium/vitamin D$_3$ supplement. This is especially important during periods of rapid growth or egg production. During these times, juveniles and females, respectively, will require larger-than-normal amounts

of calcium for healthy bone formation and eggshell production. Dust the feed insects three times a week in these cases. To dust, simply put the feed insects into a small jar or plastic bag along with the supplement, and shake them so the powder clings to the insects. If their diet is calcium deficient, geckos will often eat sand (which *could* possibly result in impactions).

Food Insect Care

You must feed your gecko healthy insects. A poorly fed or otherwise unhealthy insect offers little but chitinous bulk when fed to a reptile or amphibian. Feeding your geckos healthy insects is an important first step in maintaining the lizards in good health. You should "gut load" your crickets before you feed them to

Nose to nose with an adult albino fat-tailed gecko.

your lizards. This means feeding the insects an especially healthy diet just before they themselves become a meal for your geckos. Feed the insects grated apples, carrots, broccoli, squash, and fresh alfalfa and/or bean sprouts. Also feed them honey and vitamin/mineral-enhanced (chick) laying mash. If you prefer, several brands of commercial cricket gut-loading foods are available. Most insects eat rather continuously and will lose much of their food value if not fed for just a few hours.

If available in suitable sizes, all species of crickets are ideal for gecko food. Gray crickets (*Acheta domesticus*) are bred commercially and are available at bait and pet stores or from commercial cricket breeders. You can breed black crickets, *Gryllus pennsylvaniacus*, yourself. You can also collect them in small numbers beneath debris in fields, meadows, and woodlands.

Crickets will be cannibalistic if crowded or underfed. They get much of their moisture requirements from fruits and vegetables, but will also appreciate a water source. Since they drown easily if given a dish of water, put a few wet cotton balls into a shallow water dish (a plastic jar lid works well) or place a sponge, pebbles, or aquarium gravel into their shallow water dish. This will enable the crickets to climb out if they fall in.

Unless food is available for them, do not leave crickets in your gecko's cage overnight. The insects can be both predaceous and cannibalistic. You can safely leave mealworms in the cage at all times.

In Europe and Asia, where they are commercially available, grasshoppers and locusts (*Locusta sp.* and *Shistocerca sp.* in part) are widely used as reptile foods. Neither are commercially bred nor readily available in the United States; however, you can easily collect grasshoppers by deftly wielding a field net in fields or gardens not treated with insecticides. Grasshoppers are fast, and you may need to hone your netting skills. You may wish to remove the grasshoppers' large hopping legs before you place these insects in with your geckos.

Some indications show that the large, slow, colorful grasshoppers called lubbers contain toxins (at least in their colorful nymphal stages) that may be fatal to lizards that eat them. Do not offer these to your geckos.

The beehive caterpillar pest known as the wax worm (*Galleria mellonella*),

This striped fat-tailed gecko is of normal wild coloration.

the larval stage of the wax moth, is commercially available from bait stores and some pet stores. Check the ads in any reptile and amphibian magazine for wholesale distributors. Buy these in small numbers and refrigerate them. Wax worms have a high ratio of phosphorus to calcium, which alters the normal level of calcium in the gecko's blood. Offer wax worms as only an occasional treat.

Giant mealworms, *Zoophobas sp.*, are the larvae of a South American beetle. You can keep and raise them in quantity in shallow plastic trays containing 1 inch (3 cm) or so of sawdust. Place chick-starting mash, bran, leafy vegetables, and apples atop the sawdust for food. Giant mealworms are less easily bred than common mealworms. If you need only a few, buying them is probably more economical (and certainly less bothersome) than breeding them. If your gecko is healthy, this is one of the foods you can leave in your gecko's cage at all times. Having food readily available is a good way to maintain your gecko's weight. Giant mealworms are less chitinous than common mealworms. If you are concerned about chitin levels for your gecko, offer giant mealworms and crickets more than common mealworms.

The common mealworm, *Tenebrio molitor*, is a well-known and readily available food source. They are easily kept and bred in plastic receptacles containing a 2- to 3-inch (5 to 8 cm) layer of bran (available at your local livestock feed store) for food and a potato or an apple for moisture. You can also leave them in your gecko cage continuously.

Although no one likes raising or handling them, nymphal roaches are also an excellent food for leopard and fat-tailed geckos. Some hobbyists keep and breed giant roaches, *Blaberus sp.*, or Madagascar hissing roaches, *Gromphadorhina sp.*, both because the insects are interesting and because they are fine lizard food. Owning these imported roaches may not be legal in your state; check with your Department of Agriculture. Roaches will eat virtually any kind of healthy food, from cereals to fruits and vegetables. (Remember, to be of benefit to your gecko, the feed insects must be healthy and nutritious.) You should also provide roaches with a water source.

Mealworms are an easily procured food item that is relished by most geckos.

Health

Veterinarians and Gecko Health

Not all veterinarians treat reptiles. We suggest that you find a suitable veterinarian before your leopard or fat-tailed gecko gets ill. Check the yellow pages of your local phone book, ask your dog's or cat's veterinarian for a referral, ask at the local zoo, or check in the classified sections of reptile-oriented magazines for the reptile-qualified veterinarian closest to you.

Skin Shedding
All lizards shed their skin. The growth rate and overall health of your specimen will have much to do with the frequency with which it sheds its skin. The newly formed skin is also a more efficient moisture barrier than the old skin. The process results from thyroid activity. A day or two prior to shedding, the colors of your gecko will appear to fade. As the old keratinous layer loosens from the new one forming beneath it, your gecko may take on an overall grayish or silvery sheen. When shedding has finished, your specimen will be as brightly marked as it was previously. Both the leopard and the fat-tailed gecko generally eat their shed skin.

Although wild geckos seldom seem to have problems shedding, some captives may. Shedding problems may often be associated with newly imported specimens, in specimens that are dehydrated or in otherwise suboptimal condition, or when the relative humidity in the gecko terrarium/cage is too low. Shedding problems are most often associated with toes and tail tips, where, if not then manually (and very carefully) removed by the keeper, their adherence and drying in place can result in toe or tail tip loss. If patches of skin adhere, a gentle misting with tepid water may help your gecko rid itself of the pieces.

Skin Infections
Skin infections may be the result of excessive humidity or substrate moisture in the terrarium, or unclean substrate. Remember at all times that leopard geckos are arid-land lizards and must be kept dry. These lizards require a desert terrarium, not a river tank. African fat-tailed geckos in their savanna terrarium benefit from the bit of extra moisture afforded by their bark or cypress substrate (or by a very occasional misting if you are using sand substrate). Normal substrate cleanliness is also necessary.

Toe Loss
Unshed skin on your gecko's toes can dry and constrict the digits, causing toe loss in a rather short period of time. There is not normally any bleeding or infection associated with this, but, if it does happen, the toe stump

Healthy geckos, such as this normally colored fat-tail, usually shed their skins in large patches. The skin is often eaten as it loosens.

should be kept clean and sterile until fully healed. Applying a liquid bandage like Liquidskin will help keep the toe clean until it heals. Normal observation of your gecko during its shedding cycle will do much to assure that such trauma does not occur.

Broken Limbs

Broken limbs and other physical injuries can occur if your gecko is dropped, if it falls from any moderate height, or if it is trapped beneath a shifting piece of heavy cage furniture. If the break causes debilitation, see a veterinarian at once.

Quarantine

To prevent the spread of diseases and parasites between geckos, you should quarantine every new specimen for a given period of time. A week is the minimum time, a month is much better. During this time, each quarantined gecko should be in a cage by itself. You should carefully sterilize your hands after handling the new gecko(s) and any equipment you may use between cages. During quarantine, take the time just to watch your lizard(s). During this time, fecal

exams should be carried out to determine whether or not endoparasites are present. For this, you simply take a fresh stool sample to your reptile veterinarian. The quarantine area should be completely removed from the area in which you keep other reptiles, preferably in another room.

Thoroughly clean and sterilize the quarantine tank(s) prior to introducing the new lizard(s). Regularly clean each tank throughout the quarantine period. As with any other terrarium, a quarantine tank should be geared to the needs of the specimen it will

The prominent whorls on the tail and lack of expanded digital discs are common to the family Eublepharidae.

This is a beautifully colored and patterned young adult albino leopard gecko.

house. Take into consideration temperature, humidity, size, lighting, and all other factors. Only after you (and your veterinarian) are completely satisfied that your new specimen(s) is healthy and habituated should you bring it near other specimens.

Parasites

Many geckos, even those that are captive bred and hatched, may harbor internal parasites. These may cause bloody stools or other intestinal discomfort. Because of the complexities of identifying endoparasites and the necessity both to weigh specimens to be treated accurately and to measure purge dosages correctly, the eradication of internal parasites is best left to a qualified reptile veterinarian. It is important to use the correct medications and correct dosages, especially since geckos are such small creatures.

Stress

Any number of unsuitable caging or handling practices can cause stress. Stress can rapidly cause a decline in the health of and/or the death of otherwise healthy geckos. The single most frequently encountered stress-causing situation occurs when groups of geckos are maintained together but not provided with sufficient hiding places or sufficient food. With either species, no more than a single male can be kept within an enclosure, but he can be kept with up to two females. Both leopard and fat-tailed geckos need to have a few mealworms in their cages at all times (mealworms must be replaced with fresh mealworms daily—otherwise, they offer no nutritional value).

Leopard Gecko Dominance and Hierarchies

The importance of the dominance factor and keeping only fully compatible geckos in groups cannot be overemphasized. The actions by more dominant geckos that cause subordinate geckos stress are often very subtle—the merest nod of a head, a tail wag, or a lengthy, direct stare. If a communally kept gecko begins to lose weight or to exhibit unusual behavior (such as persistent prowling), immediately remove it from the group and house it separately.

Two males can never be housed together. A male and a superfemale (a female hatched from an egg incubated at too high a temperature; these females have many male behavioral characteristics) may clash. Superfemales may clash with other females. Sometimes, hierarchies of normal females can prove debilitatingly stressful to the most subordinate females.

In captivity, as in the wild, the strongest or wiliest male leopard gecko will become the "commander of the barracks." Other males will then have no room. The alpha male can, however, usually be maintained with up to several females.

Even the females set up hierarchies, but they are usually less aggressive in maintaining their status in a colony. If only two females are kept together, they may squabble. Several females can usually be kept together without mishap, but they should be watched. If severely dominated, a lizard may continually cower, refuse food, and soon succumb.

Fat-tailed geckos are more solitary than leopard geckos. They do well as single specimens or in trios of one male and two females. If you do keep a trio, make sure that no single member lacks a hiding place and that all are eating. If one is "going skinny" and losing weight, set up a separate cage for it, and feed it heavily.

Handling

Leopard and fat-tailed geckos are somewhat more tolerant of being handled than many other lizard species,
but they are certainly not fond of being restrained. Lizards consider being restrained as being dominated.

We urge you to consider a gecko's reluctance to being handled before you acquire your lizard and not afterward. We suggest that you keep leopard and fat-tailed geckos for their beauty and interesting terrarium demeanor rather than in hopes of them being pets you can handle and caress.

Should you have to handle your leopard or fat-tailed gecko, you can use one of three ways. All should be done with extreme care. You may grasp the lizard gently behind the head by using your thumb and forefinger. Then cup (and immobilize) it with the remaining three fingers, and finally lift it. As an alternative, you may simply shoo the lizard gently onto the upturned palm of one hand, cover it with the free hand, and lift it. Third, you can easily shoo the gecko into a cup or can and move it that way. No matter the method used, be sure the gecko is not dropped or does not jump when you are handling it. Should an accidental fall happen, internal injuries and/or broken bones may occur.

A portrait of an adult albino striped fat-tailed gecko.

Colors, Patterns, and Sizes

Is the keeping of reptiles and amphibians merely a fad? Many nonenthusiasts have felt that way. Many others (often parents of enthusiasts) have hoped it to be so.

However, reptile keeping has persisted in the face of seeming adversity. In fact, for the last several decades, it has strengthened and expanded from the simple (or not so simple) keeping of these creatures to the keeping and breeding of them. Of course, not all species of reptiles and amphibians have stood the test of time. Those that have, though, have enjoyed a popularity that only a few years ago could not have been fathomed by even the most avid of enthusiasts. Among these long-term hobby survivors, the leopard gecko is a success story of note.

The Leopard Gecko

In the early days of the hobby, before the early 1970s, back in the days when a leopard gecko was a leopard gecko was a leopard gecko, all of these lizards were collected from the wilds of primarily Pakistan. From the collection point, these pretty, black-spotted, straw-yellow lizards (designer colors were not known then) were exported to various countries where hobbyists quickly learned several facts about them. They were affordable, easily accommodated, hardy, very long-lived, and handleable. This suite of characteristics was impossible for hobbyists to overlook. Slowly at first, and then with increasing frequency, the keeping of leopard geckos caught on. As their popularity grew, leopard geckos became available in chain store pet departments and in dedicated pet stores.

Soon both private and commercial hobbyists learned that along with all of its other positive aspects, the leopard gecko was rather easily bred and the eggs were not difficult to hatch. The first few generations of leopard geckos looked much like the parents. The hatchlings were strongly barred with black against a ground color of yellow or yellow-orange. At this early stage in their lives, the baby leopard geckos looked very similar to the diminutive banded geckos of the genus *Coleonyx* that are indigenous to arid regions from southwestern United States to northern Central America. As the little leopard geckos grew, the black bands first became irregular. Then, as adulthood was reached, the dark bands fragmented into spots and occasional bars. At that point in their growth, leopard geckos began to resemble the reticulated gecko of Texas's Big Bend region and the Switak's banded gecko of both extreme southern California and the Baja Peninsula. (These two larger geckos are also of the genus *Coleonyx*.)

Untold generations of normal-appearing leopard geckos were hatched before the first color and

Although of muddled lineage, these geckos display super snow qualities.

pattern anomalies appeared. Among other happenings, the ground color brightened and/or markings faded or were of altered appearance. If the anomalies proved replicable through selective breeding, some were named. Others were just referred to by the breeders as pretty geckos or very pretty geckos. When albino leopard geckos spontaneously hatched from randomly produced eggs, using Punnett squares became the order of the day. Punnett squares allow breeders to predict what genetic combinations will arise when the genotypes (genetic makeup) of the parents are known. At that point, selective breeding programs truly became fine-tuned.

Several commercial breeders of leopard geckos are in the United States. The two with which I am most familiar are The Gourmet Rodent (Bill and Marcia Brant) and Ron Tremper. Although both facilities breed thousands of leopard geckos annually, each has its own philosophy about naming the offspring.

At the Brants' facility, the vast majority of the geckos are simply referred to as normal, pretty, prettier, and very pretty. The purchaser can call the lizard whatever he or she wishes. On the other hand, at the

Tremper breeding facility, you will find descriptive names, such as snow albino, emerine, emerald, bandit, four-eyed, A.P.T.O.R., and R.A.P.T.O.R. (among others). Note that the determining characteristics of some color phases of the leopard gecko are more readily visible than those of others. Additionally, colors, especially muted colors, are often more readily seen on live, in the hand, leopard geckos than in photographs. To confuse the color phase and pattern issues further, some names are not yet entirely standardized. Many leopard geckos now have such a mixed genetic lineage that predicting the appearance of the progeny may be all but impossible.

	Father	
	R	**r**
R	RR	Rr
r	Rr	rr

Mother

This is an adult banded hypo tangerine designer leopard gecko. The term "hypo" (short for hypomelanistic) indicates the lack of black pigment.

The following describes some of the available color and pattern variations of the leopard gecko. Although the prices of some have dropped considerably, as of late 2008, many of the more newly developed morphs are still very expensive.

Colors

Three terms, hypomelanistic, melanistic, and albino, will be seen time and again in discussions of leopard geckos. The first of these, hypomelanistic, simply indicates a reduction of the black pigment normally present in a leopard gecko. Hypomelanistic does not mean an absence of black. Hypomelanism (often expressed simply as hypo) can occur on geckos of any body color.

Melanistic refers to the black pigment, the melanin. Since no fully melanistic (all-black) leopard geckos have yet been developed, the term is often used (in error) to describe a dark leopard gecko—one having more than the normal amount of black pigment.

Strangely, the incubation temperature of a leopard gecko's egg has been shown to alter the amount of dark pigment present in the hatchling. The hatchlings that emerge from eggs incubated at warmer temperatures are paler than those hatched from eggs incubated at cooler temperatures.

The third of the three terms, albino, is discussed on page 34.

Many leopard geckos are described by their predominant colors (including eye color) or patterns. Although straw-yellow to gold is the most common body color, these lizards are now selectively bred for a rich orange body color as well as for white and green. The orange ones are referred to as tangerine leopards, the whites as blizzards and snows, and the green as emerald. At the moment, this latter description is a bit of an exaggeration.

The eyes may be gold (often with prominent black or red veining), black, or red. A rather newly developed eye color is half-black and half-gold or half-red and half-gold (in the same eye).

Yellow Forms

On some of the yellow-bodied leopard geckos, either the tail or the head is a deep tangerine orange. These are marketed respectively as carrot-tails or carrot-heads. Occasional examples may

These two super-snow leopard geckos were produced by The Gourmet Rodent.

have both the head and tail orange. If the leopard geckos have both, they are named simply by combining the two terms of carrot-head and carrot-tail.

White Forms

Pure white and off-white leopard geckos, as well as pale yellow and pale orange, all with or without darker markings, do exist. Named varieties among these are the snow, the super snow, the blizzard, and the blazing blizzard leopard geckos. All are beautiful, and all are a bit different from each other.

Both as hatchlings and as adults, snow leopard geckos are ghostly pale replicas of a normal leopard gecko. They are white with the typical charcoal dorsal spotting and light eyes. The snow albino morph was attained by crossing an albino Mack super snow with a Tremper snow albino. The eyes are black. Hatchlings and juveniles of this interesting morph are of particularly faded colors and pattern.

Lavender

Lavender of variable intensity is frequently seen as a band color on hatchling and juvenile leopard geckos. However, only those that retain the color at adulthood are referred to as lavender.

Blizzard Forms

As a juvenile, the golden-eyed blizzard morph is a solid white. At all ages, it lacks markings. Adults tend to darken a bit, assuming a dusky hue over all dorsal surfaces. The super blizzard incorporates albinism into the equation and is therefore even a purer white. Occasional examples may be a very pale yellow. It, too, has golden eyes.

A hatchling snow albino is more faded in appearance than a hatchling of a "normal" albino leopard gecko.

This blizzard morph of the leopard gecko was produced at The Gourmet Rodent.

Emerald and Emerine

Emerald and emerine leopard geckos offer a new (and still developing) color to hobbyists. The green coloration, first noted in 2004 at Ron Tremper's facility, is still pale. As the designation of emerald suggests, there is hope that

This adult emerald leopard gecko has defined green on the body. The gene for green on the body was created by Ron Tremper in 2004.

Here we have a morph of leopard gecko
known by an acronym, the A.P.T.O.R.
(Albino Patternless Tremper Orange).
This gecko is similar to the R.A.P.T.O.R.
but lacks red eyes.

selective breeding will bring increasing
intensity to the color. Currently, the
green hue appears in a dorsolateral
lineate pattern. The beautiful emerine
leopard gecko, the result of a cross of
the emerald and tangerine bloodlines,
appeared in 2005.

Other Forms

At times, a designated name is so cum-
bersome that an acronym is better. This
is the case in the next two gecko morphs.
A.P.T.O.R. stands for albino, patternless,
Tremper, orange. R.A.P.T.O.R. stands
for red-eyed, albino, patternless,
Tremper line, orange.

The A.P.T.O.R. is a beautiful,
orange-colored leopard gecko. Anteriorly, the tail often has white tubercles.
However, the tail may be entirely white
distally. There may or may not be a
deeper orange carrot-head. The eyes
are gold. Except for the eyes, which
may be entirely red or only half-red
(rather than gold), the R.A.P.T.O.R.
morph is similar to the A.P.T.O.R.
When the eyes are only partially red,
they are known as snake eyes.

The interesting eclipse morph of
the leopard gecko has a solid ruby red
eye. As in the R.A.P.T.O.R. morph, the
pupil cannot be distinguished from
the iris.

Patterns

At one time, patterns were simple.
Juveniles were banded, and adults were
spotted. Today, the available patterns
on leopard geckos are as complex as
the regimen of colors. The genetic
makeup of leopard geckos may be varied and uncharted. The breeding of a
pair of rather dull leopard geckos can
occasionally result in remarkably
beautiful colors and/or patterns that
may or may not fit any currently
described variations. Conversely, the
breeding of a pair of pretty geckos can
result in progeny that are very run-of-
the-mill in color, pattern, or both. For
many of these, the naming method
used at The Gourmet Rodent breeding
facility—normal, pretty, and prettier—
is fitting. Since it provides a compari-
son of sorts, this informal method
may even be the best.

Stripes

Dorsal and dorsolateral stripes are
among the patterns most sought by the
breeders. Stripes may appear on geckos
of any ground color and can themselves
be of many colors. Stripes are usually
complete and even edged. Occasionally,
though, they may have ragged or zigzag
edges or be interrupted by the ground
color one or more times along their
length. Among other colors, the stripes
may be white, green, tangerine, yellow,
reddish orange, or lavender. A dorsal
(vertebral) stripe of one color may be
edged by dorsolateral stripes of a sec-
ond color. Currently, efforts are being

The baldy (referring to no spots on the head) morph can occur with any number of color and pattern combinations. A baldy often has a carrot-colored tail.

made at intensifying the green (emerald) and red striping.

Baldy

As you might imagine, the Baldy morph was named for the lack of markings on the head. It was developed and named at The Gourmet Rodent.

Jungle

The dorsal pattern of this attractive leopard gecko consists of irregular, fragmented dark bars, spots, or partial bands. The ground color may vary from yellow through tangerine.

The best high yellow jungle phase leopard geckos have bold, high contrasting markings on a bright yellow ground color.

Bandit

This gecko has a strongly contrasting irregular jungle pattern. It takes its name from the bridle-like dark bar (the mask of a bandit) stretching from eye to eye across the top of the snout.

Four-eyes

The geckos designated as four-eyes have a pair of dark, outlined ocelli (eyespots) posterior to the eyes.

Polka Dot

As might be surmised, the polka dot pattern occurs when the dorsal stripe is fragmented.

Patternless "Leucistic"

Leucistic in name but not in actuality, this morph appeared in the 1990s. Although breeders now refer to this morph as the Murphy patternless, pet stores and casual hobbyists are still

inclined to refer to it as leucistic. Hatchlings have well-defined, discrete dorsal and lateral spots or blotches. These fade with increasing age. Adults are truly patternless.

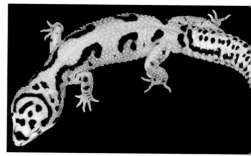

The "bandit" morph, so called for the dark band across the nose, is a variation of the jungle phase. It should have high contrast and clean markings to be of top quality.

Ghost

The ghost pattern is well-defined at hatching. It fades with increasing age and is visible but faded at adulthood.

Enigma

Some examples of the enigma morph may look exactly like a normal specimen from the wild. However, when at its best, this morph might alternatively be called a calico leopard gecko. Spots, blotches, and bars of one or two darker colors are randomly scattered over the dorsal and lateral surfaces.

Albino (Amelanistic)

If you are expecting a creature as white as a white rat when you think of the term albino, you will probably be disappointed when you see an albino leopard gecko. They simply are *not* white. In fact, several strains of albinism have now been developed in this lizard. Although each is a bit different than the next, most albinos retain visible, although usually faded, patterns. Those that do not show a

A portrait of an adult albino leopard gecko produced at The Gourmet Rodent.

pattern have been bred for not only albinism but for an additional characteristic as well.

As mentioned earlier, incubation temperature affects the color of leopard geckos. Simply stated, cooler incubation temperatures produce darker hatchlings than do warmer temperatures. Although by definition albino leopard geckos either lack melanin entirely (tyrosinase negative, T−) or lack the ability to synthesize the melanin properly (tyrosinase positive, T+), incubation temperatures affect the color of an albino as surely as they do nonalbinos. When incubated at a temperature in the low 80s°F (25s°C), albino leopard geckos emerge from the eggs banded with brown against a yellow ground color. Sometimes they are as dark as chocolate but are never black! Those incubated at a temperature of 88 to 90°F (31 to 32°C) are pale lavender against yellow. Even as an adult, if a light-colored albino is kept cool, its color will often darken. The color differences can be striking and are often lingering.

Albinism is expressed differently in the several available strains of albino leopard geckos. For example, when an albino from Mark and Kim Bell's line is bred to an albino from the Tremper

These enigma morph leopard geckos were being offered by a vendor at the 2008 Captive Breeder's Expo in Daytona Beach, Florida.

line, the resulting offspring are of normal, not albino, appearance. However, the progeny of such a breeding are double recessive for albinism. When selectively linebred to each other, albinos will occur.

Other Patterns

Two of the prettiest of the albino leopard geckos are the sunglow albino that was first seen in the late 1990s and a patternless albino. When adult, the tangerine example is just that—an overall brilliant tangerine color on its back and sides but with a white belly and white blotches on the carrot-colored tail. As an adult, the patternless albino is a warm, pale yellow with a white tail. The eyes are gold with red veining. Besides these two morphs, albino jungles, stripes, ghost, and wild pattern are known.

Size (Gigantism)

Size alone distinguishes the giant leopard gecko morph. Color and pattern are not affected. Ron Tremper identified this morph in 1996 when one hatched at an overall length of 4.5 inches (11.5 cm) and proceeded to attain a heavy-bodied adult length of 11 inches (28 cm). Tremper has termed it "the St. Bernard of geckos." The super giant trait was the first codominant genetic mutation found in leopard geckos.

Giant leopard geckos can have either one or two mutated alleles. Both giants and super giants grow slowly but often reach a size larger than that of a normal leopard. They are both apt to be of slender build.

This is a very pretty striped normal fat-tailed gecko.

The Fat-Tailed Gecko

Like the leopard gecko, the hatchling fat-tailed geckos are much more brightly marked than the adults. The hatchlings are eye-catchingly banded with dark brown against a ground color of rich buff or yellow buff. By the time the lizards are a year old, these colors have dulled noticeably. The availability of a few leucistic and albinistic fat-tailed geckos several years ago fueled an immense resurgence in commercial interest in this species. Almost overnight, dozens of selective breeding programs came into being. The leucistic trait is now firmly established; however, a steady supply of fat-tails with an albinistic trait seems to be an elusive goal.

Despite this resurgence of interest in color and pattern, there remain essentially two pattern morphs of the fat-tailed gecko: the banded and those bearing a white middorsal stripe.

The available colors—and in some cases, the prices—are what have increased.

The following lists 1999 prices for the fat-tailed gecko in its different colors and morphs.

- Normally colored fat-tailed geckos, banded pattern, hatchling $20–$30; adult $40
- Dorsally striped, hatchling $30–$50; adult $50–$60
- Khaki $300
- Striped khaki $450
- Leucistic $1,750
- Striped leucistic $2,000

More choice in color is available than in pattern. Obviously, though, the two are inextricably linked.

Banded

As mentioned, the banded phase of the fat-tailed gecko is the one most commonly seen. Common adult colorations vary from a ground color of rosy tan, tan, pinkish tan, or orangish tan to khaki, across which runs two broad, white-edged, deep brown bands. Additional dark bands occur on the prominently annulated original tail. If the tail is regenerated, it will be smooth scaled (nonannulated), will often be bulbous, and may have only indistinct banding. The crown of the head is deep brown edged with white. The specimens with the brightest and most contrasting colors are, of course, most in demand.

Some fat-tailed geckos have laterally shortened dark bands, or the bands contain light centers. Those with the most diverging bands are said to have starburst or sunburst patterns.

Khaki

The khaki phase of the fat-tailed gecko has a rather dark, greenish ground color. It also has dark brown (suffused with the barest blush of greenish pigment) bands. Seemingly, the khaki coloration is most in demand not for the morph itself but for the brightness of the whites that it produces when bred into the leucistic strain of fat-tailed gecko.

Tangerine

A very few fat-tailed geckos with a bright orange ground color, some with a suffusion of orange on the dark banding, are now being produced. The overall effect produces a startlingly pretty gecko.

Striped

Although these geckos bear a single light (buff to white(ish)) vertebral stripe that divides the bands mid-dorsally, the geckos are actually as strongly banded and as variably colored as the banded phase fat-tails. Only the presence or lack of the vertebral stripe distinguishes this phase. As with the banded morph, the juveniles of the striped fat-tails tend to be a little more brilliantly colored than the adults. The vertebral stripe of the juveniles is often best defined anteriorly.

Leucistic

Unlike the leucistic leopard gecko that seems just pale and sparingly marked, the leucistic phases of the fat-tailed gecko are spectacular. Leucistic fat-tails developed from fawn or normally colored stock have a ground color of creamy yellow with cross bands of almost pure white. Those leucistic fat-tails outbred to khaki or other stock with a dark ground color have a white ground color and banding with a translucent opalescence. The leucistic fat-tailed geckos seem to continue to pale somewhat as they age.

Breeding

Sexing Your Gecko

You can determine the sex of a reproductively active leopard or fat-tailed gecko with ease. This is accomplished by comparing the areas immediately anterior and posterior to the cloacal opening (anus). To do so, you must grasp your lizard (firmly yet gently) and turn it upside down. Male leopard and fat-tailed geckos, especially those that are sexually active, have a chevron-shaped (apex anterior) series of enlarged preanal pores as well as a proportionately bulbous tail base. The swollen area is formed by the hemipenes. These characteristics are smaller or lacking on females.

Breeding

Several stimuli, either artificially produced or naturally occurring, trigger breeding responses. Three of the most important are photoperiod, temperature regime, and good body weight of the female.

Leopard Geckos

Although the breeding season for leopard geckos may vary slightly according to latitude, photoperiod, and care regimen, it usually encompasses a seven- or eight-month period

that may begin from late in the autumn (in the deep South) to early in the spring (farther north).

The term *photoperiod*, of course, describes the length of daylight versus darkness. Perhaps as much as any other natural phenomenon, photoperiod triggers the inner workings of reptiles and amphibians—especially those that are of temperate origin and either wild caught or just a generation or two removed from the wild. Photoperiod may be somewhat less important to a leopard gecko that has been captive bred and hatched for numerous generations; however, following a natural photoperiod whenever possi-

Leopard gecko eggs incubating on a bed of Perlite at The Gourmet Rodent.

At hatching albino leopard geckos are significantly paler than a normal leopard gecko hatched at the same temperature.

ble seems best. This involves providing lessened hours of cage lighting during the short days of winter and gradually lengthening the hours as spring advances. To accomplish this, simply plug your lighting system into a simple timer, and adjust the hours of daylight weekly to coincide with the times of sunrise and sunset in your area. Concurrently, you should provide cooler cage temperatures during autumn and winter and warmer temperatures in the spring and summer. In the wild, the lengthening of the days combined with the warming temperatures signal the leopard gecko that breeding time has come.

In captivity, the period of cooling need not be lengthy. For our leopard geckos, we provided a rest period of 30 to 60 days sometime between mid-November and mid-January. Our breeders would begin producing

eggs in February and continue to do so periodically until August or September. Joe Hiduke of The Gourmet Rodent in Gainesville, Florida cools their breeder leopard geckos in September, reactivates the heat tapes late that month, and has the first eggs of the season by mid-October. Some breeders claim that no period of cooling is necessary.

If you are striving for maximum egg fertility, we suggest that you consider providing at least a short period of cooling. The cooling need not be particularly significant. Our colony had summertime cage temperatures varying from 82 to 85°F (27.8 to 29.4°C) at the cool end of the cage to 92 to 95°F (33.3 to 35°C) over the heat tape. (Note the thermal gradient!) The cage temperatures were a few degrees cooler at night. During the winter months, the heat tape was turned off. The gecko cages varied from 70 to 78°F (21.1 to 25.6°C) during days to 65 to 72°F (18.3 to 22.2°C) at night. During the period of cooling, while the leopard geckos' metabolism was at its slowest, we lessened the amount fed to each gecko.

The pattern of this hatchling Murphy patternless leopard gecko will fade rapidly as the gecko ages.

When the heat tapes were again activated, feeding was also increased. In addition, a higher percentage of pinky mice was incorporated into the diet. (Marginally fat female geckos lay more clutches of healthier eggs than thin females do.)

Breeding takes place a short time after the longer day regime begins. A male will approach a female, waggle his tail, and if the female is receptive, will place his body alongside hers. He may grasp her neck in his mouth to keep her in position. She will elevate her tail over his and gape her cloaca. He will then insert his closest hemipenis into her cloaca. They will separate after the sperm are transferred.

These juvenile banded geckos are in a sizing container. The substrate is calci-sand.

Fat-tailed Geckos

Although the basic breeding regimen for fat-tails is much the same as for leopard geckos, preconditioning fat-tailed geckos for breeding seems more necessary. Before you begin shortening the day length or providing winter cooling for your fat-tailed geckos, be certain that they are in excellent condition.

Follow the guidelines described for leopard geckos on page 38, but increase the cooling period to about 60 days. Many successful breeders of fat-tailed geckos also suggest separating males from females both during hibernation and after breeding. However, since we successfully bred fat-tailed geckos maintained communally for many years, we do not believe separation is as important as cooling, photoperiod, and topnotch health.

Once the fat-tails have been warmed following their winter cooling period, they must receive heavy feedings. Besides the regimen of crickets, mealworms, and other insects, you should offer female fat-tailed geckos a rather high percentage of newly born (pinky) mice.

Egg deposition: Once the females are gravid (the outlines of the developing eggs can usually be readily seen), provide an egg deposition receptacle. If only one or two females are gravid, you can nestle a small receptacle, such as a low (2 inch; 5 cm) margarine cup containing barely moistened sand or vermiculite, into the sand in one corner of the tank. Although females will seldom fail to find and use this, you can make it particularly attractive by hiding it beneath a strongly curved piece of cork bark. If several females are gravid, use a larger container, such as a plastic shoe box. Bury it in the cage substrate so the females can climb in easily. Cover it by replacing the lid, into which you have cut or drilled a 2-inch (5-cm) -diameter entry hole. To prevent any eggs from being damaged by females digging to find the perfect deposition spot, remove all eggs daily and place them into a temperature-controlled

Making Your Own Incubator _____

Materials needed:

1 wafer thermostat (obtainable from feed stores; these are commonly used in incubators for chicks)
1 thermometer
1 Styrofoam cooler—one with thick sides (a fish-shipping box is ideal)
3 wire nuts; electrician's tape
1 heat tape
Sturdy welded wire to make a shelf

Bend the welded wire into a U-shaped shelf. Cut the electrical cord off the heat tape, leaving about a foot of electrical cord on the tape. Make a hole through the side of the cooler, and pull the electrical wire through. Make a hole through the lid of the Styrofoam cooler, and suspend the thermostat from the inside. Attach the heat tape and the electrical cord to the thermostat by using wire nuts and/or electrician's tape. Coil the heat tape on the

incubator. Healthy female leopard and fat-tailed geckos may produce four to seven clutches of two eggs each at three- to four-week intervals.

Egg incubation: Incubation duration varies with temperature (shorter when warmer) but will probably average about 55 days. You can successfully use a number of incubation media, including sphagnum, peat, sand, perlite, and vermiculite. All need to be moistened. The laying medium we preferred was a barely moistened perlite (a 1:1 ratio of perlite to water works well) about 1 inch (3 cm) in depth spread evenly in an empty 1-pound (0.45 kg) margarine container. The eggs may be laid on their sides atop the medium or be buried about halfway in a shallow depression. Use care and do not rotate the eggs on their longitudinal axes when moving them.

While the soft-shelled eggs of the leopard gecko are not difficult to hatch, incubation is somewhat more exacting for the fat-tails. The moisture content of the incubation medium must be neither too dry nor too wet. A mixture of six parts perlite to four parts water by volume (or until barely moist) generally provides the proper moisture content in the medium.

The goal in monitoring the moisture content of the medium is to keep the eggs turgid, allowing neither the desiccation nor the overabsorption that will cause the death of the embryo. Experience will truly be your best teacher for determining your incubation techniques. Most breeders also place a shallow dish of water into the incubator to assure a relative humidity close to 100 percent.

Incubation temperatures: Rather than being genetically determined, the sex of leopards and fat-tails (and many other species of lizards) is determined by the temperature at

bottom of the incubator, making sure that it does not cross over itself. Place the wire shelf above it (this holds the receptacle of eggs above the heat tape). Add another hole in the lid for the thermometer so you can check on the inside temperature without opening the top. If the thermometer does not have a flange to keep it from slipping through the hole in the lid, use a rubber band wound several times around the thermometer to form a flange.

Put the lid onto the cooler, and plug in the thermostat/heater. Wait half an hour, and check the temperature. Adjust the thermostat/heater until the temperature inside the incubator is about 83 to 86°F (28.3 to 30°C). The L-pin handle on the top of the thermostat is the rheostat.

Once you have the temperature regulated and the wire shelf in place, put the container of eggs inside the incubator and close the lid. Check the temperature daily, and add a little water to the incubating medium as needed. Keep the hatching medium of vermiculite or perlite damp to the touch but too dry to extract any water when squeezed by your hand.

which the eggs are kept during the first trimester of incubation.

- Ideally, leopard and fat-tailed gecko eggs should be incubated at temperatures of 84 to 87°F (28.9 to 30.6°C). Within those parameters, both sexes will be produced.
- If the incubation temperature is 83°F (28.3°C) or below, females will mostly be produced.
- If the eggs are incubated at 88 to 90°F (31.3 to 32.2°C), the sex ratio will be skewed in favor of males.

Although embryo mortality often occurs when eggs are incubated at temperatures above 90°F (32.3°C), if the eggs survive, females will again be produced. However, these will be large, robust, aggressive superfemales that appear and act more like males.

Hello to the world! A leopard gecko emerges from the egg.

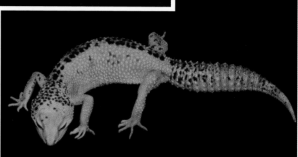

The pattern of this leopard gecko is the result of crossing a patternless "leucistic" with a normally patterned wild morph.

Although it is impossible to physically determine the sex of your hatchling leopard or fat-tailed geckos if the incubation temperature was either cooler or warmer than optimum, you can make a rather precise guess of the gecko's sex.

How do you know if the eggs are fertile? By the end of the first week, those eggs that are not fertile will usually turn yellow, harden, and begin to collapse. Those that are fertile will remain white and turgid to the touch. Since eublepharine gecko eggs do not stick to each other, remove and discard infertile ones as you notice them.

At the end of the incubation period—which may vary between 50 and 60 days—the baby geckos will cut a slit in the egg with an egg tooth on the tip of their snout. The babies often do not seem eager to leave the egg. They will cut a slit,

look out, and decide to stay inside the egg for a while longer, perhaps as long as a day and a half. When they leave the egg, the babies can be removed to another terrarium. They will begin eating within a few days.

Many breeders put each baby gecko into its own container for the first week or so, along with a few small crickets, until they are certain that the hatchling is feeding. All hatchlings can then be moved to their own terrarium, where they can be fed until they grow large enough to be placed with other geckos. Your extra geckos can be maintained within your own collection, or you may wish to sell them to your local pet store or to members of your local herp society. Whichever route you choose, producing viable young is a clear sign that you have mastered the basics of keeping leopard or fat-tailed geckos.

Glossary

Ambient temperature: The temperature of the surrounding environment.

Annulations: Whorls of scales (as on a leopard gecko's tail).

Anterior: Toward the front.

Anus: The external opening of the cloaca; the vent.

Arboreal: Tree dwelling.

Autotomize: The ability to break easily or to cast off voluntarily (and usually to regenerate) a part of the body. This occurs with tail breakage in lizards.

Brille: The clear spectacle that protects the eyes of lidless-eyed geckos.

Caudal: Pertaining to the tail.

Cloaca: The common chamber into which digestive, urinary, and reproductive systems empty and that itself opens exteriorly through the vent or anus.

Crepuscular: Active at dusk or dawn.

Deposition: As used here, the laying of the eggs.

Deposition site: The spot chosen by the female to lay her eggs.

Dorsal: Pertaining to the back; upper surface.

Dorsolateral: Pertaining to the upper sides.

Dorsum: The upper surface.

Fracture planes: Softer areas in the tail vertebrae that allow the tail to break easily if seized.

Genus: A taxonomic classification of a group or species having similar characteristics. The genus falls between the next higher designation of family and the next lower designation of species. *Genera* is the plural of genus. The generic name is always capitalized when written.

Gravid: The reptilian equivalent of mammalian pregnancy.

Hemipenes: The dual copulatory organs of male lizards and snakes.

Hemipenis: The singular form of hemipenes.

This new and beautiful morph developed by Ron Tremper in 2005 resulted from the combining of an emerald with the tangerine leopard gecko. Its appearance necessitated the coining of a new color term, "emerine." This is an adult.

The Murphy patternless leopard gecko (this is an adult) was originally and still is incorrectly known as a "Leucistic." Developed in 1993, it was first hatched by Pat Murphy and is a unique genetic recessive, which rarely combines with any other morphs' genes. It is a true patternless gecko.

Juvenile: A young or immature specimen.

Lamellae: The transverse scales that extend across the underside of a gecko's toes.

Lateral: Pertaining to the side.

Melanism: A profusion of black pigment.

Middorsal: Pertaining to the middle of the back.

Midventral: Pertaining to the center of the belly or abdomen.

Nocturnal: Active at night.

Oviparous: Reproducing by means of eggs that hatch after laying.

Poikilothermic: A species with no internal body temperature regulation. The old term was cold-blooded.

Posterior: Toward the rear.

Preanal pores: A series of pores, often in the shape of an anteriorly directed chevron, and located anterior to the anus.

Saxicolous: Rock dwelling.

Serrate: Sawlike.

Species: A group of similar creatures that produce viable young when breeding. The taxonomic designation that falls beneath genus and above subspecies.

Subcaudal: Beneath the tail.

Subdigital: Beneath the toes.

Subspecies: The subdivision of a species. A race that may differ slightly in color, size, scalation, or other criteria.

Terrestrial: Land dwelling.

Thermoregulate: To regulate (body) temperature by choosing a warmer or cooler environment.

Thigmothermic: Pertaining to a species (often nocturnal) that thermoregulates by being in contact with a preheated surface such as a boulder or tarred road surface.

Tubercles: Warty protuberances.

Tuberculated: Pertaining to tubercles. Warty scalation.

Tympanum: The external eardrum.

Vent: The external opening of the cloaca; the anus.

Venter: The underside of a creature; the belly.

Ventral: Pertaining to the undersurface or belly.

Ventrolateral: Pertaining to the sides of the venter (the belly).

Note: Other scientific definitions are contained in the following two volumes:

Peters, James A. *Dictionary of Herpetology.* New York: Hafner Publishing Co., 1964.

Wareham, David C. *The Reptile and Amphibian Keeper's Dictionary.* London: Blandford, 1993.

Helpful Information

Herpetological Societies

Individuals who enjoy reptiles and amphibians will find kindred spirits in clubs, monthly magazines, and professional societies and at pet stores, with specialty breeders, and in herp expos. Herpetological societies (or clubs) exist in major cities in North America, Europe, and other areas of the world. Most have monthly meetings. Some publish newsletters. Many host or sponsor field trips, picnics, and other interactive functions. You can often learn about these clubs by searching the Internet and by querying pet shop employees, high school science teachers, university biology department professors, or curators or employees at the department of herpetology at local museums and zoos. Inquiries and new members are welcome.

Two of the professional herpetological societies are

Society for the Study of Amphibians
    and Reptiles (SSAR)
Dept. of Zoology
Miami University
Oxford, OH 45056

Herpetologist's League
c/o Texas Nat. Heritage Program
Texas Parks and Wildlife Dept.
4200 Smith School Rd.
Austin, TX 78744

The SSAR publishes two quarterly journals. *Herpetological Review* discusses husbandry, range extensions, news about ongoing field studies, and so on. The *Journal of Herpetology* is oriented more toward academic herpetology.

A good hobbyist magazine that publishes articles on all aspects of herpetology and herpetoculture is

Reptiles
P. O. Box 6050
Mission Viejo, CA 92690

The magazine also carries classified ads and news about herp expos.

The Internet has many good locations for information about geckos in general. Three examples (and these have many links) are *tinygiants.com/caresheet/mk/gecko.htm sazoo-aq.org/gecko.htm* and *geckoranch.com/introduction.html*

The patternless albino (this is an adult) was a difficult morph to perfect. It resulted from breeding the Murphy patternless to a Tremper-line albino. Some examples have orange on the tail.

Index